P9-DEN-972

Blackbeard

by Sue Hamilton

Visit us at
www.abdopublishing.com

Published by ABDO Publishing Company, 4940 Viking Drive, Suite 622, Edina, Minnesota 55435.
Copyright ©2007 by Abdo Consulting Group, Inc. International copyrights reserved in all countries.
No part of this book may be reproduced in any form without written permission from the publisher.
ABDO & Daughters™ is a trademark and logo of ABDO Publishing Company.

Printed in the United States.

Editors: John Hamilton/Tad Bornhoft
Graphic Design: John Hamilton/Sue Hamilton
Cover Design: Neil Klinepier
Cover Illustration: *Blackbeard's Revenge*, ©2002 Don Maitz; *Pegleg*, ©1996 Don Maitz
Interior Photos and Illustrations: p 1 *Blackbeard*, ©1996 Don Maitz; p 3 *Dead Men Tell No Tales*, ©2003 Don Maitz; p 4 Queen Anne, National Maritime Museum; p 5 *Blackbeard's Revenge*, ©2002 Don Maitz; p 6 Captain Hornigold, courtesy Andrew Graves; p 7 Blackbeard, AP/Wideworld; p 8 *Queen Anne's Revenge* model, Getty; p 9 Blackbeard actor, Corbis; p 10 1733 map, Hargrett; p 11 Blackbeard, Getty; p 12 Actor as Blackbeard, Mariners' Museum; p 13 *Blackbeard's Colors*, ©1996 Don Maitz; p 14 Flintlock, Mariners' Museum; p 15 *Swapping Tales at the Pub*, Howard Pyle; p 17 *A Fierce Duel*, Mariners' Museum; pp 18-19 *Blackbeard*, ©1996 Don Maitz; p 22 Teach's Tar Kettle, courtesy the North Carolina Museum of History; p 23 Blackbeard's range map, Cartesia/Hamilton; pp 24-25 *The Capture of the Pirate, Blackbeard*, Corbis; pp 28-29 Blackbeard's skull, AP/Wideworld; p 31 *Burying More Treasure*, Howard Pyle

Library of Congress Cataloging-in-Publication Data

Hamilton, Sue L., 1959-
  Blackbeard / Sue Hamilton.
    p. cm. -- (Pirates)
  Includes index.
  ISBN-13: 978-1-59928-758-4
  ISBN-10: 1-59928-758-7
  1. Teach, Edward, d. 1718--Juvenile literature. 2. Pirates--Atlantic Coast (North America)--Biography--Juvenile literature. I. Title.

  G537.T49H36 2007
  910.4'5--dc22
  [B]
                    2006032012

Contents

Edward Teach

In the early 18th century, one pirate rose above the others to become the most dreaded and cunning buccaneer of all time. He was known as Blackbeard, the wild-eyed pirate with the fearsome figure and evil soul. Even today, nearly 300 years after his death, his name still calls up the ghosts of fear and destruction.

Blackbeard's real name was probably Edward Teach, but some history books say it may have been Thatch, or Drummond. He was born around 1680, in Bristol, England. Little is known of his family, or his early life. One clue, however, is the fact that Teach was able to read and write, skills more likely found in people of wealth.

Teach's education in the art of seamanship began during the War of the Spanish Succession, also known as Queen Anne's War. Fought from 1701-1714, when Teach would have been in his 20s and early 30s, the war pitted England and the Dutch Republic against France and Spain over who would be the next king of Spain. The war was also fought over who would control Spain's lands, including the resource-rich colonies of North America.

Facing Page:
Blackbeard's
Revenge by
Don Maitz.
Below: Queen
Anne of England.

Teach was a member of the crew of an English ship sailing from ports in the Caribbean island of Jamaica. The captain of his ship had been given a *letter of marque*. This was an official document from the government of England that granted private armed vessels permission to capture and raid Spanish and French ships.

Many countries issued letters of marque to private ships. The licenses were an inexpensive way for governments to boost their own naval forces. Ship captains and their crews who used letters of marque were known as privateers, or "gentlemen pirates." They could legally attack ships from countries with whom they were at war, sharing the plunder, or "booty," with their own governments.

The system was ripe with abuse, however. After wartime had passed, many privateers turned to piracy, attacking whatever ships they wished, and keeping all the profits. For Edward Teach, his education in seamanship and thievery led him to that exact next step.

Blackbeard

By the end of Queen Anne's War in 1714, Edward Teach was a skilled man of the sea. After the war he led a pirate's life of violence. In 1716 he found himself looking for work on the island of New Providence in the Bahamas.

The port city of Nassau, on the northeast coast of New Providence, had a natural harbor that allowed for shallow-drafted vessels—such as sloops or schooners, often preferred by pirates—to enter easily. But the shallow water prevented larger ships—like the men-of-war used by the Royal Navy—from passing. The island also featured tall hills that allowed for easy viewing of the sea. Any enemy ships lurking offshore were quickly spied. Food, rum, and companionship were plentiful. So it was no surprise that the 60-square-mile (155-square-km) New Providence was a small but welcome habitat for pirates, buccaneers, and all manner of villainous scoundrels.

Teach soon took up with one of the pirate leaders of the island, Captain Benjamin Hornigold. Known for taking on the very best crews, Hornigold was impressed with his new recruit. Teach was a tall and swarthy man; his black beard covered most of his face. He presented a frightening and powerful image. It would not be long before his distinctive hirsute feature yielded his infamous name: Blackbeard.

Although his scary appearance, fearless nature, and commanding manner helped him become a natural leader, it was also Blackbeard's great knowledge of the sea that proved him a force to be reckoned with. He was well known for his skills as a navigator, easily directing a ship's course in battle and on the high seas.

Teach sailed with Captain Hornigold on several encounters, plundering ships in the waters of the Caribbean.

Below: Pirate Captain Benjamin Hornigold took Edward Teach as a member of his crew.

The raids were only moderately successful. The pirate captain decided they would be more effective working in consort—two ships in a pirate partnership. He put Teach in charge of 70 men aboard a single-masted, six-gun vessel.

Working together, the pirate leaders cruised the Caribbean, terrorizing and plundering in tandem. During this time, Teach gained the experience he needed to become a fearsome pirate captain. All that was lacking was his very own ship, and that was soon to come.

Queen Anne's Revenge

Above: A model of Blackbeard's flagship, the *Queen Anne's Revenge.*

In 1717, Captain Hornigold and Blackbeard expanded their pirating operations. In addition to plundering ships in the Caribbean, they also preyed on vessels sailing off the coast of North America. Governors all the way down the coast, from Maine to Bermuda to Jamaica, complained that the pirating problem had grown intolerable. The governor of Jamaica said, "There is hardly a ship or vessel coming in or going out of this island that is not plundered."

In November 1717, the pirates made their way down the coast of North America. Heading south for the West Indies, they crossed paths with a French slave ship named *La Concorde.* The 300-ton, 16-gun ship had sailed out of Africa packed with a human cargo of 516 and a crew of 75.

Headed for a slave market on the French island of Martinique, the ship's two-month trip across the fierce Atlantic Ocean was difficult and horrific. According to records filed by Captain Pierre Dosset and Lieutenant Francois Ernaut, 77 slaves and crewmen died on the voyage. Diseases such as scurvy and dysentery took their toll on another 36 sailors, leaving 23 men to sail and defend the ship.

Only 100 miles (161 km) from their destination, Captain Dosset saw two ominous ships quickly approaching them. He soon discovered they were pirate sloops filled with cannons and cutthroats. Dosset's situation was dire: he had a skeleton crew of sick sailors and only a few weapons. He had little defense against two ships of bloodthirsty pirates. After only two volleys of cannon fire from the pirate ships, *La Concorde* was forced to surrender.

After seizing *La Concorde*, the pirates sailed the ship to the small island of Bequia, just south of St. Vincent and the Grenadines. The original crew and their unfortunate slave "cargo" were placed ashore. Pirates often marooned people on islands without a second thought. But on this occasion, Blackbeard left his smaller sloop for Captain Dosset and the others on Bequia—a surprisingly generous gesture.

Blackbeard found *La Concorde* pleasing, and declared his intention of taking the ship as his own. He refitted the ship with additional cannons, increasing the firepower from an estimated 26 guns up to 40. Blackbeard then renamed the ship *Queen Anne's Revenge*. The 110-foot (34-m) transport was now Blackbeard's flagship. By the end of 1717, with a powerful ship and a crew of some 150 pirates, Blackbeard set sail into infamy.

Above: Armed and dangerous, an actor shows how terrifying Blackbeard could look.

Master of Fear

Not long after Blackbeard gained *Queen Anne's Revenge,* he and partner Captain Hornigold parted ways. By 1718, Hornigold had made up his mind to retire to plantation life in New Providence. Several months later, Governor Woodes Rogers of the Bahamas offered a King's Pardon to any criminal who promised to end their pirating career. It was a bold move to help end the plague of piracy in the area. Captain Hornigold accepted the pardon. In a twist of fate, he eventually became a pirate hunter, commissioned to find and capture any remaining miscreants. However, Hornigold never went after Blackbeard.

Blackbeard had no intention of changing his ways. In fact, he was quickly becoming one of the most feared and successful pirates of all time. The wild captain radiated confidence and power. Along the East Coast of North America, his reputation grew.

Below: A 1733 map of the East Coast of North America.

Blackbeard was big and fierce. He wore a blood-red coat, over which he slung three pairs of loaded pistols, as well as a cutlass and dagger. But while he was always well armed, he knew that fear was an even greater weapon.

The pirate captain grew his black hair long; it covered most of his face and chest. He tied colorful ribbons on the twisted ends, creating the look of a madman. He also wove slow-burning wicks of hemp cord into his hair and under his hat. Smoke from the slow-burning cords encircled his gruesome face. From out of the smoky wafts, his blood-shot eyes glowed. The sight of this snarling, evil maniac often so terrified his prey that they surrendered without a fight.

Above: An illustration of Blackbeard looking his most fearsome, with wicks of hemp cord alight in his hair.

Above: Blackbeard is armed with three pistols, a cutlass, and a dagger.

Few that sailed the Atlantic Ocean did not know of the fearsome Blackbeard. Even his pirate flag inspired fear. Deceitfully, pirates often flew the flag of their prey's homeland. When an unsuspecting ship neared, the buccaneers raised their pirate flag—a sign of impending doom. The prey then had to decide: flee, fight, or surrender.

A familiar pirate flag was the skull and crossbones, also known as the "Jolly Roger." This was a reference to the devil's nickname of "Old Roger," or a slurred version of the French words "Jolie Rouge," which meant "pretty red." This referred to the original use of a plain blood-red flag that meant "no quarter given," or "no mercy/death to all."

Blackbeard's distinctive flag had many evil symbols. A horned skeleton, signifying death or the devil, held an hourglass with a lance aimed at a red heart, dripping three spots of blood. The hourglass meant "your time is over," while the pierced, bleeding heart symbolized a violent, painful death.

Above: Blackbeard's ominous flag. Art by Don Maitz.

The raising of Blackbeard's flag no doubt filled honest sailors with fear and foreboding. Blackbeard and his foul crew hoped the flag's warning of a horrifying death would result in immediate surrender. Most pirates had no wish to engage in combat—they simply wanted to take their plunder and sail away. This is exactly what happened in many cases when ships were attacked by the *Queen Anne's Revenge.*

Aboard Ship

Tales of Blackbeard's exploits are many and varied. Some say he wasn't as violent a man as the legends portray him. He and his crew often robbed their unfortunate victims, but then set them free. Blackbeard also seemed to love the ladies; he had some 14 wives in various ports. On the other hand, many sources claim Blackbeard was indeed a madman. One of his victims, a wealthy man, refused to give up his diamond ring. Blackbeard promptly cut off the finger, ring and all.

Blackbeard never let his men forget that he might do anything, at any time. He was a fierce competitor. One day several foolish crewmen accepted a bizarre challenge. Taking pots of brimstone, Blackbeard and the men went below deck into the hold and lit the hideous-smelling containers of sulfur to find out who could stand it the longest. The tight confines of the hold filled with choking clouds of yellow gas. The crewmen soon begged for air. The hatches were flung open, and the half-suffocated crewmen staggered out, gasping for breath. Blackbeard emerged last, proud to be the winner and roaring his approval of the dangerous game.

Even those closest to him were not safe from Blackbeard's dangerous antics. Once, he quietly pulled out a pistol and shot Israel Hands, his navigator and second-in-command. The bullet entered the man's knee, crippling him for life. Some accounts say it was an accident, that Blackbeard was actually firing at another crew member. Other sources claim Blackbeard did it on purpose during a drunken game of cards. Whatever the reason, Blackbeard was not sorry that he'd harmed his own crewman. He once said that "if he did not now and then kill one of them, they would forget who he was."

Above: A run-in with Blackbeard.

Ransom at Charleston

Above: An early map of Charleston, SC.

Blackbeard's excessive pride and self-confidence quickly drew the attention of many government leaders. For some dishonest politicians, Blackbeard's activities, and the spoils they brought, were welcome. For others, however, his thievery became a source of constant irritation.

In the beginning months of 1718, Blackbeard plundered several ships. He even went head-to-head with a British man-of-war sent to capture the pirate. The HMS *Scarborough* carried 30 guns. The *Queen Anne's Revenge* and *Scarborough* battled for several hours. When neither side appeared to be winning, the two ships sailed away. At least, that is what was rumored to have happened. The captain of the *Scarborough*, Francis Hume, didn't write about the encounter in his logbook, so it may not have occured. But all Blackbeard needed was the *rumor* that the battle took place. He wanted people to think that he and his ship of cutthroats had held their own against—and even bested—the powerful British warship. Blackbeard's reputation grew.

It was around this time that Blackbeard crossed paths with another pirate, Major Stede Bonnet. Bonnet, a most unusual pirate, had been a wealthy landowner. He had purchased his own ship, and named the sloop *Revenge*. Bonnet was more of a dandy gentleman on a lark than a true pirate, although he and his crew had taken several ships. It's possible that Bonnet took to pirating mainly to get away from his nagging wife.

Whatever the reason, Blackbeard and Bonnet teamed up, although it did not take long for Blackbeard to realize that Bonnet was no seaman. Teach convinced Bonnet that the well-groomed man should not have to suffer the difficulties of being a captain.

Bonnet came aboard the *Queen Anne's Revenge* while Blackbeard sent one of his own men, a Lieutenant Richards, over to command Stede's vessel.

The two *Revenge* ships, along with two other sloops that Blackbeard had captured, soon cruised along the North American coast. With four ships and some 300-400 pirate crew members, Blackbeard's menacing fleet ended up at the port of Charleston, South Carolina, in May 1718. Here, Blackbeard made his most blatant, and ultimately foolish, pirate venture.

Above: Blackbeard battles members of the English Royal Navy.

For a week, Blackbeard's ships blocked the Charleston harbor, attacking ships attempting to enter or leave the port city. He and his cutthroats seized nine ships. They stripped the vessels of cargo, and the passengers of jewelry and money. Blackbeard even captured several hostages, including one of South Carolina governor Robert Johnson's ruling council, Samuel Wragg, and Wragg's four-year-old son.

Above: Grappling hooks anchor the two vessels together, as Blackbeard and his pirate crew climb aboard with weapons drawn and pistols raging. Art by Don Maitz.

Storing the captives in his ship's hold like so much cargo, Blackbeard chose several pirates and one hostage, a Mr. Marks, to row back to the city with the pirate captain's demands for their release. "Lay the matter before the governor and tell him to give me what I ask. Give it, or I will give him heads on a platter and burn the ships that lay before the town." Strangely, all Blackbeard demanded was a chest of medical supplies and drugs. It's a mystery why the pirate captain did not ask for money. Charleston was one of the richest port cities in the country. Many historians guess that Blackbeard may have been ill.

Blackbeard waited three days for the return boat. Luckily for the captives, who were told that each day would be their last, Mr. Marks finally returned with the chest of medical supplies.

True to his word, Blackbeard released the hostages, although not before stealing whatever wealth they had in their possession. Blackbeard then sailed away. However, his blockade of Charleston brought him to a new level of notoriety. He was now at the top of the area's "most wanted" list. But the pirate captain still had several tricks up his bejeweled sleeve.

Treachery and Deceit

After his profitable ventures in South Carolina, Blackbeard sailed with his fleet of ships to Old Topsail Inlet, in North Carolina. Sometime in mid-June 1718, the pirate captain entered what is known today as Beaufort Inlet, and ran the *Queen Anne's Revenge* aground. He then insisted that another ship in his fleet, *Adventure*, attempt to free the large sloop.

Below: Stede Bonnet was tried and hanged for piracy in 1718.

Both ships became stuck fast. This is probably what Teach had planned all along. With some 300 crew members, his treasure was spread thin. The pirate captain had no intention of sharing his wealth with so many scurvy dogs.

Teach convinced Stede Bonnet to travel to Bath, North Carolina, where the colony's governor was offering the King's Pardon to pirates. Bonnet set sail in the *Revenge*. With Bonnet and his crew out of the way, Teach took the time to strip *Queen Anne's Revenge* and *Adventure* of anything of value. He then sailed away with only 40 of his most experienced crewmen. However, the former captain of the *Adventure*, David Herriot, who had been pressed into Blackbeard's service,

Left: An illustration of Blackbeard, who was an experienced sailor, as well as a fearsome and deadly pirate.

Below: Stede Bonnet, more of a fancy dandy than a rogue, unwisely took up pirating with the wily and treacherous Captain Teach.

demanded payment for the loss of his ship. Teach's response was to maroon Herriot and 16 others on a small, sandy island.

Stede Bonnet eventually returned, with his pardon in hand, and rescued the men. But instead of ending his pirate career, Bonnet continued to attack ships. A few months later, he and several of his men were captured and hanged.

Meanwhile, Blackbeard traveled to Bath, North Carolina, where Governor Charles Eden gave Teach a pardon. Teach had been to Bath earlier in the year, in January, and received a first pardon from the governor. Obviously, Blackbeard never had any intention at that time of ending his pirate career. Now it was summer 1718. With a second pardon, would Blackbeard finally settle down and become a law-abiding member of society?

Welcoming A Pirate

Below: Teach's Tar Kettle, an oven-shaped structure that once lay in an open field near Bath, North Carolina. The brick "oven" was rumored to have been used by Blackbeard for boiling tar for calking his ships. The structure no longer exists.

With treasure in hand and a second pardon from Governor Eden, Blackbeard purchased a home overlooking Pamlico Sound, directly across from the governor's house. Some believe that Governor Eden received many payments from his friend Teach—bribes that allowed Blackbeard to steal as he pleased with little fear of punishment.

Teach married Mary Ormond, a wealthy plantation owner's daughter, who was only 16 at the time. Governor Eden officiated at the wedding. The fact that Blackbeard had at least 10 other living wives seemed not to matter.

The town of Bath welcomed Blackbeard as an exciting member of the community. His very presence in the area kept other pirates away. He generously entertained local landowners and political leaders, and received invitations to many parties and dinners in return. Teach once bragged that he would be welcomed in any home. However, Blackbeard's pirate ways were not yet over.

TEACH'S TAR KETTLE

For such a bold man, the life of a plantation owner was deadly dull. Blackbeard craved adventure and danger. From his home, he could see ships sailing by, and knew they were easy pickings.

Blackbeard finally rounded up his crew and returned to his fast sloop, which was anchored at the southern tip of Ocracoke Island.

Blackbeard started raiding vessels sailing near his home. He also intercepted a French ship sailing to Bermuda. The vessel was loaded with sugar and coca. Teach transferred the crew to his own small sloop, and kept the prize ship as his own.

After sailing back to Bath in September 1718, Teach lied to Governor Eden, reporting that his new ship had been abandoned. Eden, together with the colony's chief justice, Tobias Knight, declared that the ship's contents should go to Blackbeard, and that the ship should be burned—thus making it impossible to trace its origin. For their parts in the deception (since all parties knew quite well that the ship was in fact stolen), Governor Eden received a handsome bribe of 60 barrels of sugar. Knight received 20 barrels.

Blackbeard's illegal activities were once again in the public eye. Many citizens and political leaders were quite unhappy. His week-long party with fellow pirate Charles Vane in October of that year added to rumors that Blackbeard's intent was to continue robbing honest merchantmen. This, plus the fact that the pirates seemed to be building a fort on Ocracoke Island, was the last straw. It was time for action. With the knowledge that Governor Eden would do nothing against the pirate, Governor Alexander Spotswood of Virginia took matters into his own hands.

No Quarter Given

In the fall of 1718, Virginia's assembly posted a reward for Blackbeard—dead or alive. Governor Alexander Spotswood of Virginia leased two sloops, the *Ranger* and the *Jane*. The smaller ships were needed in order to enter the shallow channel surrounding Blackbeard's hideout at Ocracoke Island.

The highly secret mission was placed under the command of a Royal Navy officer, Lieutenant Robert Maynard, who led 35 men on the *Jane*. The smaller sloop, *Ranger*, carried 25 men under the command of another officer, Midshipman Hyde. Both Maynard and Hyde were brave sailors with plenty of experience. At dusk on November 21, 1718, the two sloops approached Ocracoke Island and spied Blackbeard's new ship, *Adventure*, anchored offshore.

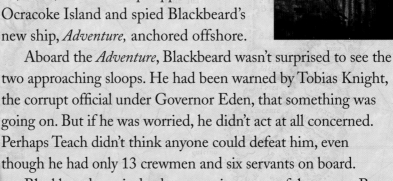

Aboard the *Adventure*, Blackbeard wasn't surprised to see the two approaching sloops. He had been warned by Tobias Knight, the corrupt official under Governor Eden, that something was going on. But if he was worried, he didn't act at all concerned. Perhaps Teach didn't think anyone could defeat him, even though he had only 13 crewmen and six servants on board.

Blackbeard was indeed an amazing, powerful seaman. But Lieutenant Maynard had his orders, and a large reward awaited

if he and his men could successfully capture the notorious pirate. As Teach drank and sang long into the night, Maynard readied his troops for battle.

Above: Blackbeard battles Lieutenant Robert Maynard of the Royal Navy.

As the night wore on, Blackbeard's pirate crew became alarmed. They asked Blackbeard if his wife, Mary, knew where his treasure was buried, in case something should happen to him. Teach responded, "Nobody but me and the devil knows where it's hid—and the longest liver will get it all."

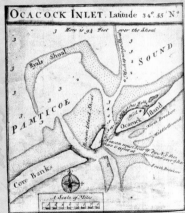

Above: An early map of Ocracoke Island, NC. Blackbeard met his doom in the shallow waters surrounding the island.

When morning light dawned, Lt. Maynard hoisted the Union Jack and immediately set sail for Blackbeard's vessel. Blackbeard was forced to cut his anchor cable to escape. He shouted across the waters, demanding that his adversaries identify themselves. Maynard responded, "You may see by our colors we are no pirates."

Blackbeard had no intention of surrendering to these "cowardly puppies" of the king's men. He bellowed, "…seize my Soul if I give you quarter, or take any from you!"

If Maynard was frightened by the pirate legend, he did not show it. He coolly shouted back, "I expect no quarter from you, nor shall I give any!"

As the two sloops approached, they suddenly ran aground on the shallow bottom. Blackbeard had a great fighting advantage because he knew the ins and outs of the narrow channel. Plus, his ship was armed with cannons, while Maynard's ships had none.

Eventually, the two sloops were freed by the rising tide. Since the wind was too light to use the sails, the sailors rowed toward Blackbeard's ship. The pirate responded with cannon fire. The broadside attack killed Midshipman Hyde and five of his men aboard *Ranger*, which was forced to end the attack. Half of Maynard's crew aboard the *Jane* were also killed.

Maynard ordered most of his crew below deck, except for two seamen who sailed the ship. Blackbeard was completely fooled into thinking he could easily capture the sloop. But as soon as he and his boarding party were aboard the *Jane*, Maynard and the rest of his men rushed out of the hatches and attacked. Blackbeard fired at Maynard, but missed. Maynard returned fire, shooting straight into the pirate's chest. Still, Blackbeard fought on, bringing his cutlass down so forcefully it broke Maynard's sword.

Maynard appeared doomed, but just then one of his men struck Blackbeard in the neck with a broadsword. The pirate bellowed, "Well done, lad." The sailor, a Scotsman Highlander, replied, "If it be not well done, I'll do it better."

As the *Boston News Letter* later reported, "With that he have him a second stroke, which cut off his head, laying it flat on his shoulder."

Maynard reported that Blackbeard fell to the deck "with five shot in him and 20 dismal cuts in several parts of his body." The rest of the pirates fought desperately until the remaining crew of the *Ranger* approached. By then, the deck of the *Jane* was red with blood and the bodies of the injured, dead, and dying.

Maynard hung Blackbeard's head from his ship's bowsprit as gruesome proof of the brave lieutenant's successful mission. Blackbeard's body was tossed overboard. As legend tells it, the headless corpse swam three times around the ship before finally sinking to its cold, watery grave.

Above: Blackbeard's head swings from the bowsprit of Maynard's ship.

Golden Age of Piracy

With the death of Blackbeard and the following trials and hangings of his crew, plus that of Stede Bonnet and his fellow pirates, the Golden Age of Piracy was finally winding down. It was a relief to a great many honest sailors and merchants.

Some 300 years later, Blackbeard's legend lives on. Books, games, plays, and movies have been created surrounding the master of fear. Many tourists travel to the North Carolina coast, intent on visiting the area where the infamous pirate lived his last days. Many holes have been dug in vain in search of his missing treasure. It has never been found.

However, treasure of another kind was discovered in 1996. The *Queen Anne's Revenge*, Blackbeard's flagship, may have been located in Beaufort Inlet, North Carolina. Not everyone agrees that the recovered wreck is Teach's ship. But several artifacts—including a bronze bell dated 1705, plus a collection of different-sized cannons, which a pirate ship would be expected to have—lead archaeologists to believe that this shipwreck is indeed the *Queen Anne's Revenge*.

Interest in Blackbeard has never faded. The man created such a fearsome image for himself that he is still remembered, even without having to "kill a crewman now and again." A notorious captain and a master of the sea, Blackbeard lives on in legend.

Above: Blackbeard's skull? Acquired from
a collector by the Mariners' Museum in Newport News, Virginia, this
grisly artifact is believed to be the remains of the notorious pirate.
After Blackbeard's death in 1718, his severed head was placed at the
mouth of Virginia's Hampton River as a warning to other pirates.

Glossary

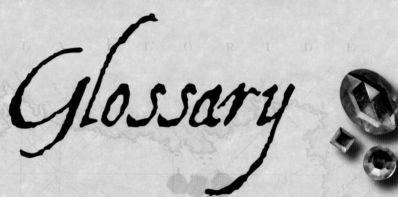

Bahamas
A group of islands in the west Atlantic Ocean, southeast of Florida and north of Cuba. Held as a British colony in the 18th and 19th centuries.

Booty
Money, jewels, and other valuables seized off a ship by raiding pirates.

Bribe
An offer of money or other valuables made in order to sway someone's actions. Often made to government officials to stave off arrest.

Buccaneers
Men who raided and captured ships, especially off the Spanish coasts of America during the 17th and 18th centuries.

Caribbean
The islands and area of the Caribbean Sea, roughly the area between Florida and South and Central America.

Cutlass
A short, curved sword having a single sharp edge, often used by sailors.

Dagger
A knife-like weapon with a handle and pointed blade.

Dysentery
A disease of the stomach and intestines marked by diarrhea; caused by infection.

Flagship
The largest and most important ship in a fleet. Also, the ship that the commander of a fleet sails on.

Letter of Marque

Official government document granting a ship captain permission to use his personal armed vessel for capturing and raiding ships of another country. Used by governments to expand their naval forces at a time of war.

Navigator

The person in charge of plotting and directing the course of a ship.

Pirates

Rugged outlaw seamen who capture and raid ships at sea to seize their cargo and other valuables.

Privateers

Ship captains and crew members who operate under a letter of marque, attacking and raiding ships from countries that are at war with their own country. Also known as "gentlemen pirates."

Schooner

A two-masted sailing ship, easily maneuverable and able to navigate shallow waters.

Scurvy

A disease resulting from a lack of vitamin C in the body, often due to an insufficient amount of fruit in the diet. Symptoms include general weakness and bleeding gums.

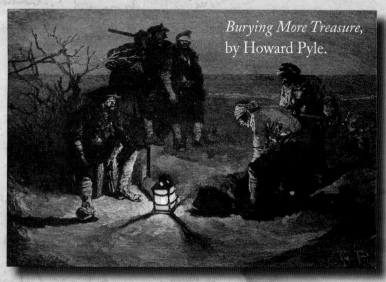

Burying More Treasure, by Howard Pyle.

Sloop

A fast sailing vessel with a single mast. Outfitted for war, a sloop had a single gun deck with 10 to 18 cannons.

Index

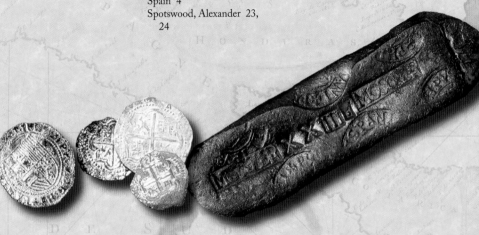